MARTIN HONEYS[...]

D0130439

Fit for Nothing

How to survive the health boom

CENTURY PUBLISHING COMPANY
LONDON

First published in Great Britain in 1983 by
Century Publishing Co. Ltd,
76 Old Compton Street, London W1V 5PA

Reprinted 1983

ISBN 0 7126 0236 4 (paper)
ISBN 0 7126 0235 6 (cased)

Printed in Great Britain in 1983 by
Richard Clay (The Chaucer Press) Ltd.,
Bungay, Suffolk

Compared with our ancestors, modern living makes far fewer demands on our bodies...

When I was a lad we had to walk to school without shoes.

— driving around in cars,

I've felt so much better since I started pushing the car to work each morning.

sitting at the office desk all day,

He's been doing that for three years and he's still a seven stone weakling.

watching television all night.

He calls it aerobic TV watching.

It's no wonder our bodies become weak...

*He's done nothing but moan about his aching arm
since the electric toothbrush broke down.*

and without a proper diet become fat.

It was probably being overweight that killed him.

Fortunately, more and more people are becoming aware of the need to keep fit.

When I realised I couldn't touch my toes I decided to do something about it.

Although you might think you get enough exercise as it is...

He's taken up darts because he thinks all the walking will do him good.

— taking the dog for a walk,

He still pulls hard but I'm used to it now.

gardening...

*The nice thing about gardening is that the better
at it you are, the fitter you become.*

or doing the housework doesn't use every part of the body.

I pay you to clean, Mrs. Marshtwit, not to keep fit.

Complete exercise is needed, encompassing the three factors required for physical fitness...

Typical of him, he has to do everything at once.

Why can't you hold the W.I. weightlifting class in someone else's house for a change?

suppleness...

What's the point of being fit if you can't even go out for a walk when it's a bit windy?

and stamina.

You've no stamina, Henry, that's your trouble.

You can make a start by changing your daily routine — use the stairs instead of the lift...

First he started using the stairs instead of the lift, then that became too easy.

or walk instead of taking the bus.

There goes what used to be the 8.47 No. 15.

But to achieve higher levels of fitness,

Is that washing dry yet?

a more strenuous form of exercise is needed...

Quite honestly, I don't know why you bother.

— such as jogging,

*Jogging's done me a lot of good — I can get to the
pub ten minutes sooner.*

which many people have taken up in recent years...

No, it's not a marathon, there's a job been advertised at one of the factories.

Isn't he a bit young for jogging?

from all walks of life.

Everyone's jogging-crazy these days.

You can jog almost anywhere,

I'm not warning you again, Dobson, you do your jogging in your own time.

You're not going out jogging in this weather?

without the need for special equipment…

He likes jogging but he's embarrassed about being seen.

— although good running shoes are a must.

Yes, these will do fine.

Jogging is an aerobic exercise...

and aerobics...

Aerobics? No, he's just practising kicking down doors.

are very fashionable at the moment.

*So much for his aerobic services boosting
attendance.*

Aerobic exercise increases the amount of oxygen taken in by the body,

Now and then she goes out to recruit new members.

thus exercising the heart and lungs.

I know he looks fitter, but I still say walking was more dignified.

Aerobic dance...

Quite honestly, Miss Fenshaw, I don't think you need do both the dance and the body-building class.

and keep fit classes...

Could one of you stretch by the door – there's a terrible draught coming in.

are opening up all over the country,

*If you've come to see about the job, take a squat
over there.*

though it is best to check beforehand...

Yes, Fiona, you have a question?

which ones are suitable.

*You'd think they'd have the beginners' class on
the ground floor.*

Some instructors might not be fully qualified...

and push you too far.

*It's all right – Jennifer has reached the 'burn'
stage.*

Check your pulse regularly...

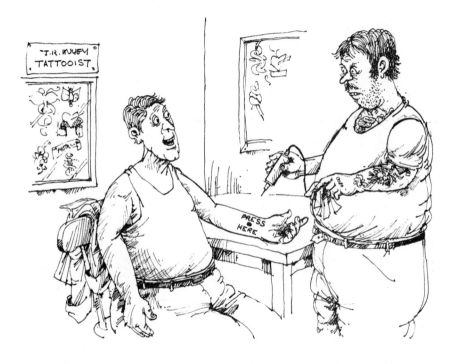

Thanks – I always have trouble finding my pulse.

— you don't want to overdo it.

*It's best to take it easy to start with, so I suggest
you just watch for the first week.*

The idea is to work up a good sweat.

Wear comfortable clothing...

Has anyone seen Sonia's other leg warmer?

and, once again, make sure that you have a good pair of shoes.

You'll find these extremely well-cushioned, sir.

You don't, of course, have to go to classes for your aerobic work-outs...

He's selling home exercise courses.

— you can do it just as easily at home.

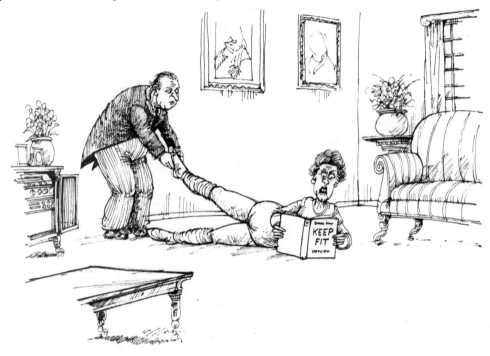

Now lift the other leg up and down ten times,
Jenkins.

There are numerous books, records and tapes available...

Thank goodness you're home – the record's stuck.

**which, provided the instructions are
followed carefully,**

*According to this, you're not supposed to do your
back in until page 83.*

will prove just as beneficial.

She swapped our table for a cassette player.

Swimming...

It's not the swimming in the bath I object to, it's the diving off the edge.

and cycling are also good forms of exercise.

Sometimes I cycle to work — and then sometimes I don't.

Public baths are cheap to use...

Personally, I think your mother's spending far too much time at the swimming baths.

and accessible to most people,

As it is, by the time I've got here I only get ten minutes in the water before I have to get back to the office.

while the roads are free to cyclists once you have the equipment.

I can't really say it's cheaper—I spend as much on oxygen as I used to spend on petrol.

If you buy a bicycle, it's important to make sure it's the right size...

That bicycle I bought the other day — could I trade it in for a larger one?

and that the saddle is comfortable.

If this doesn't work you'd better take up jogging.

You don't have to go outside — exercise cycles are just one example...

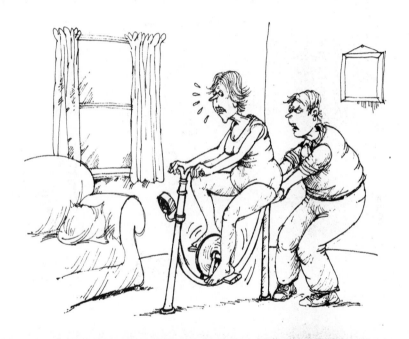

I wish you'd bought the de-luxe model with a stand.

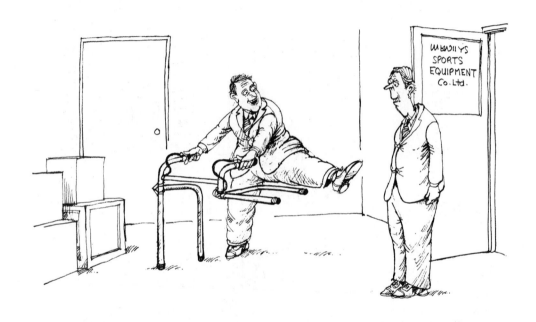

This is our latest design – something for the more elderly keep fit fanatic.

to keep fit in the comfort of your own home.

He says it feels more like real rowing if he's getting wet.

However, if you want to be healthy and lead an active life,

She'd rather exercise at this bar than the one at the dance class.

Vitamin pills haven't kept her young, they've kept her positively juvenile.

is just as important as physical exercise.

She's obsessed with weight watching.

You can't be fit if you're fat...

The trouble is, I can't get close enough to read it.

— and while exercise will help you lose weight,

He eats the same amount but this way he burns it off quicker.

you might need to lose weight before you can exercise.

It's not the box we can't get through the door, it's Harry.

So many people are overweight these days…

It's amazing really – after all these years of marriage you can still make the earth move for me.

— though many of them are anxious to lose some of it.

She really is desperate to lose weight.

For some, it's no problem,

It doesn't matter what he eats, he never seems to put on weight.

He has *helped me reduce my desire for food, I must say.*

There are many diets and slimming aids available in magazines and books...

or you can make up your own.

It's her self-imposed diet — she only eats what she can find.

Some are more effective...

As diets go, it was rather drastic.

*She cheats really – she goes and buys herself
larger clothes.*

High fibre diets are very much in the news these days.

Fibre diets are all very well, Mrs. Dobbs, but there's such a thing as overdoing it.

In modern refined foods, the fibre is taken out...

It's not the unrefined food I object to, it's the way she serves it up.

and research has shown that low fibre diets...

can cause bowel problems,

It's all the white bread people keep giving them.

diseases…

Stop moaning – at least it's not contagious.

and tooth decay,

*The vet says I've been giving him too many
sweets and biscuits.*

whereas high fibre diets, apart from being good for you,

Look, I don't mind eating potatoes with their skins on, but I'm not eating chips with their wrapping on.

need more time to chew…

I won't have any dinner tonight – I'm still eating breakfast.

and are more filling,

One bean or two?

thus helping you to slim.

*If you don't eat your greens you won't grow up to
be a little man.*

Bran and beans have a high fibre content,

It's amazing what she can do with a can of beans.

although they can cause flatulence.

I blame the craze for high fibre diets. Who needs substitutes when they can have the real thing?

Vegetables, too, are high in fibre...

I don't mind you having a picnic but you could at least bring your own food.

and vegetarianism, once regarded as a crank cult,

We're all strict vegetarians in this house.

is becoming more and more popular.

He's a vegetarian now but he still likes going shooting now and then.

For those who find dieting difficult,

She's resisting temptation.

there are health farms,

*You'll find we're great believers in carrot juice
here, Mr. Thompson.*

electronic trimming aids...

or, as a last resort, you can have your jaws wired up...

She keeps trying to suck cream cakes through her straw.

or have excess fat removed surgically.

I still say they've taken too much off one side.

It's well known that smoking can affect your health.

All that talk about 'stunting one's growth' is pure rubbish.

It's not easy to stop,

Do you like our wallpaper? It's to help us stop smoking.

but you'll feel a lot fitter if you do.

With a cough like that it's not surprising you have trouble putting your teeth in.

You'll also save money...

*With the money I save through not smoking I can
buy myself an extra bottle of gin each week.*

and find that food tastes a lot better.

I never realised how awful her cooking was until I gave up smoking.

Anti-smoking clinics can help,

I can assure you, after you've smoked one of these you'll never smoke again.

as can hypnosis...

He does very well out of it – he never has to buy his own cigarettes.

and acupuncture,

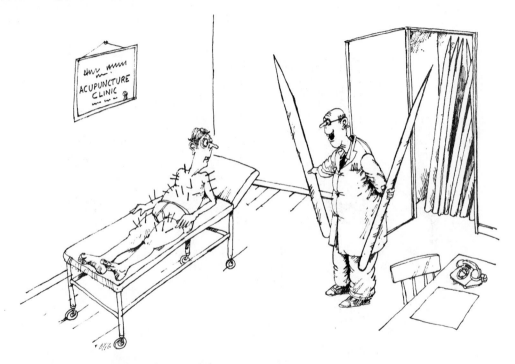

*If that doesn't work, we find the next phase is
usually effective.*

but in the end it really depends on your will-power.

No thanks – I'm trying to give them up.

There are other aspects to good health...

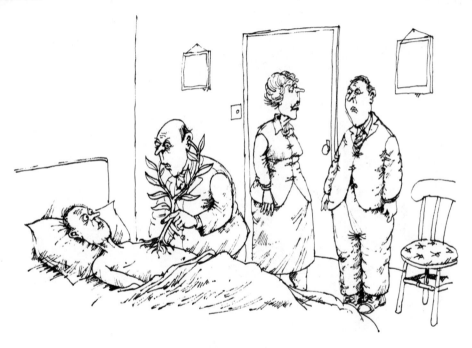

Dr. Sprout is a great believer in herbal medicine.

— yoga keeps you fit...

I hope I'm not interrupting anything?

and incorporates relaxation...

I wish you'd do your deep breathing exercises somewhere else.

and meditation, which helps combat stress.

They both have different ways of relaxing – Mum meditates and Dad vegetates.

But whatever form of exercise you use, and it's important to find the method that suits you best,

Your artificial snow has arrived.

you'll find that being fit will give you a fuller,

It not only keeps him fit, it cuts down our electricity bills as well.

They're both keep fit fanatics.

and, probably, a longer life.